The Fossil-Box

Richard Marggraf Turley

Published by Cinnamon Press
Meirion House, Glan yr afon, Tanygrisiau,
Blaenau Ffestiniog, Gwynedd LL41 3SU
www.cinnamonpress.com

The right of Richard Marggraf Turley to be identified as author of this work has been asserted by him in accordance with the Copyright, Designs and Patent Act, 1988.
© 2007 Richard Marggraf Turley ISBN 978-1-905614-35-6
British Library Cataloguing in Publication Data. A CIP record for this book can be obtained from the British Library.

All rights reserved. No part of this publication may be reproduced, stored in a retrieval system, or transmitted in any form or by any means, electronic, mechanical, photocopying, recording or otherwise without either the prior written permission of the publishers. This book may not be lent, hired out, resold or otherwise disposed of by way of trade in any form of binding or cover other than that in which it is published, without the prior consent of the publishers.

Designed and typeset in Palatino by Cinnamon Press
Cover design by Mike Fortune-Wood from original artwork by Marc Silva, 'Pentaeum with Bug'© Marc Silva
Printed in Great Britain by Biddles Ltd, King's Lynn, Norfolk

Acknowledgements:

Some of these poems first appeared in *Agenda, Poetry Wales, Planet, New Welsh Review, Cadenza, Stand, Orbis, The Wolf, Dream Catcher,* and *Equinox*. I am grateful to the editors for permission to reprint.

Stanzas from 'Blakeney' originally appeared in *Whiteout*, published by Parthian, whose permission to reproduce here is gratefully acknowledged.

I'm grateful to my friends in Aberystwyth, who commented on many of these poems.

Contents

Vorrest:

Blakeney	9
Viney Hill	18
Little Dean	26
Pillowell	28
Parkend	32

The Fossil-Box:

The Fossil-Box	39
Berries	40
The Bluetit	41
Egyptian Monologues	
1. Stonecutter	42
2. Prayer	43
3. Captain's Lament	44
4. Pharaoh's Sandal-Bearer	45
Sound and Motion	
1. Afternoon	46
2. Apple Tree	47
3. Evening Bird	48
Sunbreak	49
Llanrhystud Suite	
1. Segments	50
2. Syzygy	51
Debouching	52
Anning	53
Jumping Waves	54
Sea Jellies	55
Ode	56

Boxing the Compass	58
Aubade	59
Launch	60
Gathering	61
Ploughcrows	62
Calliphora	63
Swimming Lesson	64
The Raid	65
Giants	
1. Welsh Giants	66
2. Irish Giants	67
3. Norwegian Giants	68
4. South American Giants	69
Bears at Ruardean, 1889	70
No. 2 Voluntary Mines Rescue Brigade, Cinderford	72
Hub Caps	73
Crystals	74
Zapped	75
Stars	76
Tintern Parva	77
Seven Bridges of Königsberg	78
Plum Tree	79
Dragonfly	80

The Fossil-Box

For J.K.

Vorrest

Blakeney

1

I've returned to the forest's legerdemain,
its green conjury, for new paths
through the gravity of trees,
new treadways over the spoils

of its worked sections; to browse
the clints and grikes and thin soils
that suckled, forged character
and foible, synapse and junction.

I'm here to dig down, layer
and label, break apart.
What slips through conifer
stands across the derelict bed

of track? Deer or hare, scoped
by goshawks flapgliding
over scoriae and clinker?
Or other, older company?

2

The drive to this place is a journey
in old time, massless and unphysical
through the disused mineral loop
at Moseley Green with its ghosts

of woebegone wagons; and water-
logged routes beside the Lyd
in Norchard's gales; along the Dean
road that runs to Ariconium,

where masters smelted arms
for legions; past Staunton's stones,
the Toad, Broad, and dislodged Buck
of Buckstone Hill, and wooded

scarps where moss feathers
oolitic walls. Time dilates
like moons the half-life
of my adventure.

3

They planted squatter cottages
and low farm buildings
around meanders and tributaries
of the Wye, hidden in frames

of orchards, beech and alder
cloaking valley slopes, shelter-
belts for settled margins.
I hunker, too, in the matured

coppice, the worked wood,
beneath high supports of trees.
What slowburning, charcoal
fealty do I owe these vales

and folds, these lappetted
shales? What deep time
has leeched into the bands
and joints of rocks?

4

No name for the hewn scowles
we dared not enter, bare rents
of rock thatched with ferric
yew, drawn to the iron

in fathomed lime below.
We bounded over felled tops
and lops of commissioned trees,
kicking daddocky windfall

above the haematite pits
of New Dunn and Old Sling,
slow, elbowing ways,
into unfenced legspace,

canopied air widening
in the essential forest,
where boreal larches
nurse lea oaks into cord-

wood, through piney crests
and over rings of lamina
shale, no verderer to check
our unchartered, off-piste trails.

5

Each path along the roads
between the forest's thick
fingers registers the pull
of remote syntax.

Names like *Speech House*,
incalculably dreadful signs
of as far from home as it was
possible to go, unfeasible

miles from the slag and broken
cottages that line the Straits,
where bracken sucks
through anaemic roots.

6

It's shrinking, margins closing in
on deciduous broadleaf, already
fringed with needle and cone.
The canopy caught my fancy.

Once, fifty feet behind parents
photographing unpollarded limbs,
terror dug in deep, and I cried
for the feathered light. Later,

the sudden right hand through
the fern seemed differently
placed with each orbit of the trees
as we drove the old Austin

to the new house. Grancher
raised it with Moses, his father,
the mason. It stuck out, ashlar
faced with frogs. At the cider

press, sharp fruit, fusty hessian
and tacit time with the miner.
I didn't work at his forest burr,
making sense instinctively

of the prolonged vowels.
Over from the bays, vegetable
rainforest. Runners loped up poles;
broadbeans squat, defiant;

cabbage heads peering above
their trenches. Tucked away,
a wooden lid in the ground.
I prised at an edge with a boot,

watched the appalled heave
of worms in the vat, an endless
seam of shit, this deep working.
We spoke once, the miner and I,

of the underworld, colour TV
blaring in the bayed front room.
I asked how it was – and the Board's
long ton seemed small recompense.

I watched him haul radiant
chunks from his windowless
shed, scuttle the glossy stones
with practised whoosh

of the worn shovel, lean one hand
on the wall as if to hear the coal
again, feel the gangers' voices
in the gale, The Horse, Little Horse,

Low Fault, this friable domestic
seam. Nineteen-eighty-three,
when the forest slipped shape,
unkempt, flaking at the gable end.

7

Aunty Gwen was new to me.
I was pronounced my dad's son.
There was talk of Uncle Albert,
Grancher's brother – blew up

in the war – whose eyes and nose
I got. Their forest brogue, its slow
substance a living thing, a copse
of sound. Other words fell

flat before the corpulent
diphthongs. The village hymns
I could almost believe, slow
and ancient like ringwidths

of the forest's floating chron-
ology. Abide with me and the old
hundred of St Briavels for the free
miner. My dad sang, and I trebled.

We filed from borrowed pews –
sloped speechless under the fluent
apse to a raw plug in the earth,
a lid over ash. I drifted, relative

to their grief, felt chlorophyll
surge through the veins of trees
older even than the old butty
with his thees and thous.

8

New sheep, not born under oaks
but brought in after the cull,
don't get the forest's green
code, stroll across the resinous

white, lose themselves
in the old battle lines –
commoners and incomers,
labour and leisure.

Not sure now where I stand.
I've avoided it for years.
Redshifting from the forest,
delayed by my own momentum,

a boy seeing forms and faces
in the trees, I cast my eye
up to the hanging questions
that could be bats.

Viney Hill

1

The bungalow above the Severn
was never in the same place
twice. It jumped out from hedges,
binding wooded co-ordinates

separated by more than light
or finite space. Its uncanny
geometry: living room right
from the glazed hall,

picture window ox-bowing
in the tides; and to the left – terra
incognita, bedrooms and worse,
and passage to the teeming plot

behind the kitchen – and gardens,
hidden gardens on three sides,
flowers within flowers, fenced
by a brittle edge of beech.

One foray into the screened
zone unearthed a cart parked
on veined stones, identical
to my own, a birthday gift;

but sawn for longer legs,
long brake-lever jammed
against spoked pram wheels,
animate with meaning.

Once, I found a raised lagoon,
watched its cloudy secrets
move by stealth from reed
to reed. In those dog-days

the river dazzled along the flats,
as if some leat had drained
Dark Hill, and I felt the foundry's
smoulder on my face.

2

Winter and Gibbons,
steely iron-masters,
stripped the smelting heart-
shaped tranche of Dean,

and Villiers' wife wired off
Mailscot Wood. Always thorny,
touch and go, this rough
acreage; centuries since

the Bulley boys dug in
deep with pot-bellied pigs,
were ousted from their herbage,
made to patch the pushed-

in walls. I fancy myself
pannaged with the disgruntled
crew, loath to pay the lady swine-
silver for ancient rights;

envisage their gorgeous rout
in double-glazed vistas
out over the Severn. It took
the renegade priests of Parkend

and Berry Hill to shake lime
and loam, render the foresters'
quick cabins into homes, squat
hamlets into wildwood parishes.

3

Espionaged from the window,
the river's saline –
too wide to comprehend.
Aunty Joan sketched

the Severn bore, but
it didn't wash. What stuck
was Gerald's prophecy,
chill as elements:

They'll go for the power-
station, take us all. Empty
space till then, I looked
now at Oldbury's

capped meres, asked if
the wave would reach
the forest, prayed our oaks
might slow the heat

with fingers of deep
time. I calculated the stands
and groves as concentric
rings of ash around our home.

4

The open rhymes of Rodley
collect the Severn's
soluble tithes. Inland,
hawthorn hedge gives way

to post and wire, far from the flint
of Viney Hill. Clogged stretches,
neglected since the silting
of Lydney Pill, when the harbour

went to seed with all its ships
and navigable streams,
echoed in more recent slips,
the grounded barge at Severn Mill.

5

From the Viney road,
ways into the forest –
opening on chancels
of heartwood

hidden from themselves,
ringed with gravity,
registered by the leaf-
weathercocks of All Saints,

where I am still –
in the miner's procession,
my uncoordinated grief
graceless in the south porch.

After the service, the gathering
in the tiled kitchen,
the wife changed
for all time in her chair,

as incomprehensible
to the speechless
boychap as to the man,
as unnavigable.

Over the fence, holly
and ruined walls;
older than custom,
the forest's apsidal lines.

6

These wide renovated
spaces. Our party burrows
through karstland,
halogen beams igniting

flowstone and stalagmite,
the earth's slow movements
these standing things.
I'm here to hollow out,

free associate with the past,
channel new routes
into the present, to slough
off in these wet rocks

and groined ceilings,
ochre my face with slips
and pigments blushing
from the walls.

7

Each new journey to the hills
and scarps rewires the forest's
fuses, clears new contours
through the baffled geography,

river redshifting through
the canopy. No dead rent,
these working ways. In them
we celebrate the mass of small

things, feel again the ferrous
leach through tourist strata.
I will leave my children
in trees, let them grow

fluent in the argot of copse,
conjure henge and hammer
in these run-down grottoes.
The refurbished forest laps

at the fringes of circuit
roads, inundates shackle-
tracks, gorse embankments
still no bar to the drift of sheep.

Little Dean

1

'Dean', from Mitcheldean
or Dean Magma; or
the Saxon *dean* or *dene*,
denoting *dale* or *den*;

or from the sheltering
Danes, hiding out
in the forest's thickets
and thorny brakes.

The uncertain forest,
unfathomable, un-
knowable now as icres
of iron and broken jars,

deadpan as druidical
rocks and bones and coins
stamped with the head
of Aurelius in the scowles.

2

The forest's branch
lines, tramming it from
New Fancy to Strip-and-
at-it; and underground,

fanning out with no plans,
the deep seams, miners'
mattocks crossing,
untangling black veins

from black veins – always
a bone of contention,
these parochial ways.
Traipsing the glebe,

I come to myself, peramb-
ulating among forbid-trees,
scrambling over kibbles
and offal timber

in the fence months,
picking a route through
the six walks for ink-
lings, previews of the past

and what remains,
hearing sympathetic notes
in the antics of bread
rioters and wall breakers,

catching the drift of
Warren James, unloved
cabiner, mustering
the forest against fences.

Pillowell

1

Each causeway over the forest's swallets
and shakeholes, spoils and con-
glomerate rock, leads back
to mylnes and rooty estuaries,

the mumbo of days. I return
to pith and pathways, to the imp-
ression of trees; read back into the boy
the impending past. In my measly

childhood illnesses, the atom-
thin membrane between sensation and
nothing, ear-ache enough to pound
through and grasp the gist of what

I knew lay there. Now there are breaks
in the sympathy of branches, green
interference. Signs bend through the stage-
craft of trees, a provision of light,

an arrangement of more than memory.
I reconnoitre the knotty fringe,
see myself as waves and particles,
the forest a slow lens of tense relation.

2

Pillowell was iron and stone,
old school cloistered
beneath prolific leaves.
There was a boy, he appeared

in different forms, until one day
we left the curtilage of palings
to play under oaks and beech
blued with lichen. I ran bionically,

my voice amplified by the ring
of trees. Nothing beyond
the forest's colour wheel of chloro-
plast and rough-rendered houses.

We skirted roots and scowl-holes
into understoried pits, scuffing
the stacked foliage, the child's world
phasing behind stands of silver

birch, our small horizons
oscillating through kissing
numbers of trees. We scarpered
from foes, indeterminate shapes

conjured from layers of human
occupancy, from the calc and ferrous,
the frank blood of Dean. We darted
under the shield of xeroxed leaves

into moieties and perambulations,
tracking Cromwell's men with wooden
shovels, fossicking for ore. We watched
Lea fence straight into Free Wood,

cheered for Nurdon to yank his gate
with cart and chain; and running
further in the hills and sconces,
the forest's basin, further back

to the new, we climbed on the old
encroachment cottages, spooking
the larks at Sinkaway field; through
acres and perches to Bogo and Paunce-

foot and the plans to cut Kyllicote
Wood. We were root and stem,
signal and consequence, formalized
by the forest, left to its future.

3

Near the tangled hem that selvedges
to Lydney by the farm silos,
me and my best butty, scouting
unmetalled ridges between slurry

fields, shadowing haw-
finch and redstarts. We stalled
in the porridge of mud, profound
plane that sucked at our thin ankles,

scouring from memory even
our names. I fled, ditching boots
and Sean, calling at his door
on Templeway West, his mother

a sudden spectre. That night
the broidered shade above my bed
sent long legs scuttling over joints
of walls into spindled visions: articulate

creatures, brittle, carapaced, veined
like leaves; and I wondered if the face
in my boyish dreams and the forest's
knock-toddy were the same.

Parkend

1

The old words decay
as forest decibels
among rust fungus
and red belts

racked with drought,
bote and estover
for a fourth journey
in the mind.

At the derelict junction
down from the Viney,
Parkend's sharp right
shot into the blue

of conifers, on either
side the thoughtless
purlieu stretching
into unplottable distance.

I looked for it later
with the borrowed mini,
and couldn't be sure
it had ever occupied space

at the complicated core
of green years. It remained
a probable place, proof
of the forest's superposition.

2

Derrick cranes at Bixhead
hoist the royal blues
from chamfered beds,
bound for the frame

saws at Cannop.
Pneumatic fists drill
and crop; bevelled
rocks arrive for walls

in dumpy bags.
In the long south
aisle at Ruardean,
beneath the splayed

lancet windows,
yeoman Wansley
lyeth in hope, called
home, 58 years, 8 m, ½.

3

They wouldn't call,
afraid to wink
out of visible light
beyond the foliar edge.

Each week, we crossed
in the old Austin,
blinking from the dual
carriageway into crowds

of trees. Now I remember
that sprung gate and sloping
drive, unresolved shapes
left, back door ajar,

Dad's broad *Well?*
through the dark hall,
resonance that rose
and fell again at Staunton.

I never saw Grancher in a car.
It seems impossible now,
unfeasible as his colour
set. But in the low phaeton

to the crematory, I huddled
next to his brother Frank,
who played trombone. Small,
he seemed to shrink like a child.

4

Up from the descending semis,
Sean's nan had the forest
in her mouth, bracken
plumbing her tongue.

The straits' liquids
had changed a child's sibil-
ants to ancient
occlusive stops.

We called her Gags.
My butty said he could
understand the babble.
I'm not sure.

She was a leaf-
thing, curled in her chair,
waiting for a second
turn to take her off.

2. The Fossil-Box

The Fossil-Box

For Jacob and Jozef Olivey

They planted the perfect ammonite
among the rocks for the boys – loose

change from the fossil shop –
the guide's human eyes playing

along. It was enough to keep
the hunt going, that chiselled

afternoon. At home, the deposit-
box lies open on the table.

We pick through permineral
treasures for the impressions small

lives leave on hard objects. In one
split core of ripe stone, a maggot

of lucent crystal, coiled, or un-
coiling, its universe an inverse ratio.

Berries

A flicker of wren
flung itself from one
stem of winter hawthorn,

berries the only sign
of life on the bone frame,
to another, shouldering air

with nothing more than
momentum. Since then
the bush has trembled,

phonating with the ring,
this leftover of swerve,
and with the wind, and my

own woody junctions
register the wake. And
that is all. The spiky

sprigs are silent, the thrum
ended, and there might be
one less red gule to bend

the cold sun. Other things
break in, dislodged stones
in the dry wall, the grass

that needs trimming.

The bluetit

flutters into focus,
making a mess
of its landing, to peck
at the putty of our

inverted world, agit-
ating in old sheets
of glass, rattling sashes,
showing the endless

brown of its irides,
points of un-
mirroring light,
dimensionless, aerogel,

plotting the algebra
of flight, drawing my
unexpecting eye close,
close, its low churr

scolding or singing
or sending into
blank space notes
to the unresolved flock.

Egyptian Monologues

1. Stonecutter

Since I came into being
as flesh, I have lived
among gnats and sand-fleas,

most industrious during
the floods, not otherwise
employed in the fields.

My heart gladdened
to see stones, given
form with the float

of hands, rise with kites
and pulleys, fall
with the precision

of silence. Now the casing
shines like silver,
even the poorest can say

in words that open
ways to hearing, it has come
to an end in peace.

2. Prayer

Give me wisdom to wield
power over words,
maker of the obedient

stars. God of hidden
form, lord of flood
and sand, whose breath

is lilac, forgive me my
enemies, deliver me
from crocodiles. Silt-

deity, when I arrive
at your palaces, may you
pause before repelling me.

3. Captain's Lament

The gods are gone, fled
to their chambers who raised

the earth. I have pressed beyond
the perfumed lands to furthest

islands, returned with gifts
of cassia and cypress; wrangled

with tyrants, hunted the sand-
dweller. I have rested on the props

of heaven. Not even a king can sway
the days of being born or dying.

4. Pharaoh's Sandal-Bearer

Wielder of crook
and flail, tamer
of the speckled

serpopard, subduer
of reptiles and lord
of inundation, mirror

of the living sun, over-
seer of the limits
of land, may your life

seep like silt into
the bank of un-
rememberable dreams.

Sound and Motion

After Keats

1. Afternoon

The birds are incessantly
on the move this blue
afternoon and children tramp-

oline into trees planted
for an orchard. Out front
the big black dog lopes

after a ball; these assembled
intervals, the sine waves
of joy. She calls, grass-

hoppers stridulating
warning ahead
of my scissoring feet.

2. Apple Tree

In autumn, I will move
this apple. Now I sit
in the mask of its leaves

to learn to feel the blue
and cloudless stars vagueing
the sky. A squanderer

in slow time, I over-
hear the garden sink
into its lobes and lap-

pets. There is sympathy
here the birds communicate
like a tannoy of hearts,

a fondness exhaled
as scent, turning
through the ground.

I have planted my feet,
attuned my ears to the in-
finite whirr of wheels.

3. Evening Bird

You follow invisible
wavelengths into
that intangible space

between evening and sky,
bird I cannot name,
appearing to me first

as a shape and adding
time across a breath-
less quadrant of air.

With a tree that has expressed
apples, I listen to your reck-
less song, untranslatable,

saying all and anything;
while you braille the earth
as air under wings.

Sunbreak

that morning came to mind
under a worry of clouds,
Skirrid to the left, Little Skirrid

rhyming to the right – the light
self-contained, bisque, aureoline,
goldenrod. We pulled up short,

leaning on the car doors, and you
gave me that saying about dawn
carrying gold in her mouth.

Llanrhystud Suite

1. Segments

There are shapes rational-
ising the sky over light
waves and jellies

hanging in July water.
Swimmers postpone
everything in the

moment   stirring
the sea   the correl-
ate of shore.

Again gulls pull time-
consuming arcs,
folding the distinct air.

The scene speaks in up-
beat segments of relation.
Shore to sea. Gull to space.

2. Syzygy

Today's leaping tide tears
back the perturbed sand
to clay and through

clay tops of early forest
punctuate the strand,
xylem the bath-

ymetry of Llanrhystud.
These echelons of rubbed time
prompt to the world's

things, the bare fact
of earth's era, and shapes
in the clouds seem almost

physical on this flung
Welsh lunula. I ramble
in the warm gradient,

measuring feet to the spill.
The ground feels
its displaced gravity,

echoing crescentic jets
above the shrum of sea.
Our horizons collapse,

expand and end with
the *rawk-rawk* of gulls
clipping water.

Debouching

Some ways to break
cover. Girard's steady river
spilled from the stones
at Saint Amand –

splashed the fog saddle
jib of gun sprung-
blinking crawling in
furnaces o the
small mouths –

all facing that bright
fluid instant.

Anning

Months after I bury my father,
I dig up a monster. It rises
snapping from the marl
like a crocodile, one vast eye
fixed on the trowel.

So there's the cabinet-maker
again, fussing over my puzzle-
work, its interlocking parts.
I think of nothing to say,
give myself to the fish-lizards.

Jumping Waves

The fish in the shallows
are transparent
filaments of instinct,
the boys crystal
against the dripping sea.

They leap in crests
and shout as they skip,
lost in the joy of jumping
waves, my son and his sea-
compatriots.

The sun strikes
louder on the brass
sands, and pebbles shimmy
in heat, searing the curve
of this equidistant strand.

Still they hop and dash,
charge and retreat, scattering
drops of glee. Nothing
is not right about
their moment –

nothing not marked in marrow,
that won't be called back
before sleep, and breathe
long after; the boys,
hard at the work of play.

Sea Jellies

Patrolling the salt edge,
I stumble on a smack of jelly-
fish the colour of cataracts.

I'd thought them flimsy,
diaphanous, whether
beached or floating;

but these are callous, heavy,
rough-skinned things
severed from the sea.

Later, I learn they swarm
and bloom, live in brainless
knowledge of the light.

Ode

Gaudeamus igitur, iuvenes dum sumus.

Two of us in cagoules,
sailing into the cwm-wind. I keep
one eye on a swoop of future,
        insurgent
below the clouds. My son wears
        spiderman wellies.

We talk as we shoulder
on, cajoling the dog. The runnels
I chased as a boy were like these,
        but not as wide.
We used to trap bull'eads
        in tupperware tubs.

He has something to say
as we lean into the mud-
cambered old-road, scouting
        through concrete
farmyards. Rights of way,
        if it comes to it.

Because there's no end in sight,
ever, we turn a circuit that brings us
ponies, and the shoddy paddocks,
        up for sale since
for ever, or as long as
        we've been here.

And that's it. An hour or so on Sunday,
and something to extract. Then
tea – perhaps a bath – TV.
    Why must I tick off
the day in segments,
       finding no other way?

Boxing the Compass

You laid out the dead
plugs as a wind-
rose round the hob,

north
north by east
northnorth-east
north east by north

heating ribs, incubating
gaps in the rusty flame.

Our car's keel slipped
darkness like a cat
spitting hair.

That night we rolled
and tacked through
the city's rhumb-
lines on current, both
learning the regions of air,

Boreas
Eurus
Notos
Lips

mapping the *fleur-de-lis*
of your north.

Aubade

For K.G.

The spill of morning
over trees between
stuccoed walls and the lean

of chimneys; as if
someone's shimmied
up the rigging of

clouds, clambered through
the day's lubberhole
to a blazing gazebo,

and is pouring
pleasures of light
on a fiction of ground,

their hullooing bugling
to the warmed,
the still unstirring world.

Launch

He shuffles between
his *New Collected*
and *Posthumous Poems*

previewed in a clutch
of loose sheets.
They speak to the cross

legs and studious elbows.
At first I hear centos
of Yeats and then it

happens, something sinks
into the knots and whorls.
I find myself in love

with what this man gave
up other things for – all
these feet, the spasm

of scissored knees
a polygraph of heart-
beats. The older man

beside me fights time
with bread drenched
in olive oil. His brogue

kicks a calmer cadence
than the *redondo-dedo*
of my foot stuttering.

Gathering

Someone waits in the bed
pegged for strawberries,
lamb clutched against the spring.

Further into the fenced-off plot,
a farmer gathers the ewe
camped in our curtilage,

returning with a kicking
sack across his shoulders,
shins stopped with cord.

It's then I see my daughter
for the woman with the lamb.
At the pick-up, she cradles

her gawky beast, reluctant
to deliver; offers to feed,
keep at home for ever.

Ploughcrows

Crows that clatter behind the plough
smell the worm in the uncovered
evening, sense my small presence
       between hedges.
They follow furrows, their bearing
       to beast-machine.
I jog the field's cosine, an eye
on the fleet of birds, their slips
       and skids,
the sudden flare before the plunge.

Calliphora

Sun coaxing brimstones above hedges
has hatched bluebottles that tail me
along lanes. Our rendezvous
       is road-kill,
limbs akimbo, eyes' blind spots
       gawping at the dog-
leg that let death in – landing lights
for flies with inestimable eggs.
       Some way off –
a horn, raising the question of dust.

Swimming Lesson

We sent it screaming the length
of the pool, sanitizer fumes,
unwashed feet, mingling
in the municipal air.

I didn't see the near-
miss that upset his bath-
capped wife a boy of twelve
could tell was not quite

right as she hauled herself
and other dead weight
up the rust-flecked ladder,
her eyes full of more than

just a watery scud,
my mates melting away.
I hung in the greasy shallows,
chlorine fogging my throat,

skin ready to fall in wraps;
anything but the slow walk
to the cubicles and god
knows what.

The Raid

For Jozef Macioszek

We went in at dawn for a chicken
near Nantes. Six o'clock
is just daylight in September.
A peaceful ambush, they spared us
the bullets, dozens
of partisans lining the birch.
Some said lynch us there
and then and be done;
but they searched us first.
Polish papers saved my day,
and yours. No, the officers
didn't mind; we did as we pleased,
the enemy on all sides.
It was like being away
from home. We were young,
compared to you.

Giants

1. Welsh Giants

i

Rhita Gawr, fetishist,
made a mantle of kings'
beards, tried it on
with Arthur.

ii

It's all in the glands –
two Welsh heads
no match for Jack's
killing bonce.

2. Irish Giants

i.

The Portrush giantess rose
seven feet in shoes peat-
cutters' boots rattled in,
knew men from their peri-
wigs, stooped to shake
hands at the fair.

ii.

Quick-witted Oonagh
once salvaged Finn – nifty
fifty-footer – from the Scottish
behemoth off the Causeway,
Don't wake the baby
her legendary put-down.

3. Norwegian Giants

i.

The giant Vind
och Veder – Wind
and Weather – steeple-
jacked by holy Olaf
and his new-fangled ideas
to the tune of a new church.

ii.

Loki's mistle-
toe kiss, dashing Frigg's
hopes for beautiful
Baldur. After that,
Thokk – the first tranny –
and the long dash
to Ragnarok.

4. South American Giants

Foul-Weather Jack,
famed for the Falklands,
sailed on the Dolphin,
met several in Patagonia.
Pigafetta claimed the land
was named after big feet.

Bears at Ruardean, 1889

Wilkes of the Cinderford mob
killed the bears at Ruardean.
They fined him five pounds.
No kin of mine was listed
in the miscreant papers.

We were otherwise
employed: hodding
and hacking, nursing
charcoal stacks,
firing foundries
with Mushet's special
self-hardening steel.

The Frenchmen arrived
early on Friday, Huget,
Sirgant and Yas, two
muzzled bears in tow.
Between them they kept
the Cinderford young
amused up and down
the high street the whole
deciphered morning.

In time they reached
nearby Nailbridge,
and the old rumours:
the beasts lived
off the clandestine
flesh of dead children.

Two hundred colliers
congregated to kill
the bears in the open fields
of East Dean. The small
one they dispatched
with a pole; the larger devil
lolloped off and was shot
on the skirts of Cinderford.

And none of mine appeared
in the lists with the murderous
Wilkeses, Baldwins, Meeks
and the shameful Cinderrys.

On that road, if you listen,
without coming too close,
you can hear the drum-
head trial of the bears,
their cudgelled keepers,
the clumsy speeches
among the rusty holly-
hocks and bramble.

But we were other-
wise. No lineage links
the fuming pack
to ours and mine.
No kin listed in the mis-
creant papers.

No. 2 Voluntary Mines Rescue Brigade, Cinderford

Photograph circa 1920

Braving the flash, they perch as great ram-gods
for the picture, corrugated tubes horning from their heads,
feel the gob-stink of gas rise in the roadways,
wind through delf and dipple, branch and bronchiole.

The third on the right rubs elbows with Clifford's son,
holds his canary as though he weren't a bird-
lover, its haldane-cage a new-fanglement,
like the alkaline trick of light on his left-beat knee

and choke-damp gauge. Smoke goggles up, his face
has something mine might claim as kin. I release
the feed-gear of time, lift my handset to raise him
on the alien telephony spilling at his rough feet.

Hub Caps

The fat kid runs in huge shapes
before the sculptured steps.
His horizon pulls like this
and that, a fluid belt of ballast.
But he runs in any event,
happy to chase and never arrive.
I knew heavy boys as weight-
slingers, strong-arms. This one
is voluminous, glad to be
in the game. You're alright,
fat kid. Cheeks like hub caps.

Crystals

A new procedure of snow
cuddles the world; open
form its granular beauty.

I step out into the hoar
frost and capped columns,
rubbing poles of haw-

thorn rimed between the inch
and finger, mull the drift
of air, gradually under-

standing the chilly magnitude.
I pull my jacket close, and
possibly the snow stops.

Zapped

The rub of unlike
objects – shoe leather
on carpet, balloon
on jumper, new lovers –

there's always a charge;
20 thousand volts
is nothing, and discharge
painful. Imagine the static

on alien worlds, soils
baking under coronal heat,
crumbling to dust in thin
air, all forms of life

evaporated, snowlines
rising. I dream of missions
to proximate Mars, catching
in pixels the drift of it.

Stars

If there at all,
this spattering edge
by the fire's hem.

Our borderless worlds
are boggling glomes
of thought, shocking

expulsions, allergies
of gods; or gods
themselves, startled

from each other relentlessly.

Tintern Parva

Rembrandt in the Bronstraat
loiters at the shushing water-
wheel. His beard is magnificent,
his unrefracted eye breathes
life to the *pointillé* clientele.
The waitress speaks some English,
each syllable a new flat world.

I take in her Dutch tongue,
its chromatics, far from the bone-
mappers and wold-walkers
of Tintern, blue woods echoing
in phloem the Abbey's lopped
columns. I can't imagine
why the forest or the files

of sheep, or the Severn's cam-
bered banks or the curtain
walls at Chepstow, crop up
at this table for one in the corner.
Rembrandt – I'm sure it's he –
lopes by, brush in one hand,
perched cigarette in the other.

Seven Bridges of Königsberg

Squint and you almost see
the burghers perambulating

the Pregel banks of the city,
well-to-do, seeking the circuit

of each bridge once, once
only. Euler's solution was nothing

if not elegant: reduce landmass
to vertex, bridge to figured edge;

eliminate all features, the sum of it.
Later, two hundred Lancasters

drop five hundred tons of bombs,
remove a fifth of industry, a third

of homes, two bridges; the city
solved again, a graph of itself.

Plum Tree

The white bedroom,
shutterless,
is a hinge

between worlds.
The plum taps
at the wavy pane,

bending light
over curled limbs,
painting *shi* symbols

on your lips,
shushing the orchard's
inimitable calm.

Dragonfly

Afterwards, you un-
fold, sit drying

your wings, watching
the pupated world

with faceted eyes,
having inched ex-

hausted from exuvia.